INSISTENCE

Ailbhe Darcy was born in Dublin in 1981 and brought up there. She studied for her PhD and MFA at the University of Notre Dame in the US, and taught there and at the University of Münster in Germany. She is now a lecturer in creative writing at Cardiff University. She has published her poetry in Ireland, Britain and the US. Selections of her work are included in the Bloodaxe anthologies *Identity Parade* and *Voice Recognition*, and in her pamphlet *A Fictional Dress* (tall-lighthouse, 2009). Her first book-length collection, *Imaginary Menagerie* (Bloodaxe Books, 2011), was short-listed for Ireland's dlr Strong Award at Poetry Now / Mountains to Sea. A collaboration with S.J. Fowler, *Subcritical Texts*, was published by Gorse in 2017. Her second collection, *Insistence*, was published by Bloodaxe in 2018.

AILBHE DARCY

Insistence

BLOODAXE BOOKS

ISBN: 978 1 78037 078 1

First published 2018 by
Bloodaxe Books Ltd,
Eastburn,
South Park,
Hexham,
Northumberland NE46 1BS.

www.bloodaxebooks.com
For further information about Bloodaxe titles
please visit our website or write to
the above address for a catalogue.

Supported using public funding by
ARTS COUNCIL
ENGLAND

Cover design: Neil Astley & Pamela Robertson-Pearce.

Printed in Great Britain by Bell & Bain Limited, Glasgow, Scotland, on
acid-free paper sourced from mills with FSC chain of custody certification.

for Nicola & Raphael,
Mum & Dad

ACKNOWLEDGEMENTS

Versions of some of these poems have previously appeared in *The Battersea Review, Connotation Press, Éire-Ireland, Horizon Review, The Manchester Review, Poetry, Poetry Ireland Review, Poetry Wales, 3:AM Magazine, The Wake Forest Series of Irish Poetry*, Volume IV, edited by David Wheatley (Wake Forest University Press, 2017), and *Wordlegs*. Part of 'Postcards from Europe' appeared in my pamphlet *A Fictional Dress* (Tall Lighthouse, 2009) and in *Identity Parade: New British & Irish Poets*, edited by Roddy Lumsden (Bloodaxe Books, 2010).

This book couldn't have been written without a bursary from the Arts Council of Ireland/An Chomhairle Ealaíon, for which I'm very grateful.

I'm also grateful to Miriam Gamble, Richard Gwyn, Mark Thomas Noonan, Justin Quinn and Eoghan Wills for helpful comments on some of the poems, and to Patrick Cotter, David Wheatley, S.J. Fowler, Christodoulos Makris, the Gesicki family and Sarah McKibben – among others; I hope you know who you are – for material encouragements at crucial moments. Thank you, Chris Fox, for the Keough-Naughton Institute for Irish Studies. Thank you, Joyelle McSweeney, for introducing me to Inger Christensen's *alphabet* (Bloodaxe Books, 2000).

Thank you to friends, teachers, siblings, mentors, colleagues and students at the University of Notre Dame, Cardiff University and elsewhere, for conversations that mattered. Above all, thank you to John Harvey, who's worked almost as hard on these poems as I have.

Insistence is dedicated to my parents, who gave me the whole insistent world in the first place.

CONTENTS

❧

I shall punish the earth, I shall turn down the heat
I shall take away every morsel to eat
I shall turn every field into stone
Where I walk crying alone

Crying for Proserpina

Proserpina, come home to Mama, come home to Mama now

KATE McGARRIGLE, 'Proserpina'
(recorded by Martha Wainwright)

❧

But I'm not sure we'll ever say the world is ours again, not
sure we'll ever really feel at home here again.

JOHN JEREMIAH SULLIVAN,
'Violence of the Lambs' in *Pulphead*

Ansel Adams' Aspens

To tiny Ansel Adams, newly arrived on this earth,
the sky must seem a miracle. I'd commit the scene
to black and white if I could, the sky bright

and bottomless, trees gnarled as the knees of elephants.
Helpless in his Biltrite pram, Ansel Adams is watching
the clouds roll in. Then the clouds would gather speed,

roll out again, and the camera pan down to Ansel Adams
the man, kneeling on granite, choosing one filter
over another. It's as though more and greater apparatus

were needed to recapture that first exposure, says
the voiceover: as though Ansel Adams were a pioneer
toiling after the spirit, not just the body, of America.

To tiny Ansel Adams, newly arrived on this earth,
the sky must seem a matter of fact. It's the mind
beneath he wants to grasp, stowed in its smart black

enclosure. I'd have his pram gather speed and transform,
a cartoon robot against the heavens, wheels spinning,
into Ansel Adams' camera. Now the bright black sky

is Ansel Adams and Ansel Adams the filter;
light renders each tree a bouquet of paper;
the Great Depression gathers like so much weather.

To tiny Ansel Adams, newly arrived on this earth,
the sky is what it is, taut with its isness.
Some time before dawn, the section framed

by interior blackens and brightens and each tree out there
glows with itself, with the certainty of all Ansel Adams'
aspens. No one is watching but this one bewildered

immigrant, toiling after sleep, saturated in monochrome.
Sometimes it's all you'll find in the wilderness: Ansel
Adams, tiny in his pram, composing the day just gone.

Still

There's a picture in your head
instead of someone else's— you could hang it—
the still of that smallness— indefinite and keen—
an adult's hand— stern as a wristwatch— holding
a child in time— then it was not night— here
on the porch threatened by knotweed and all
the resources of artificial light—

An adult can hold a child like that
and not mean cruelty— just holding on
to someone small who's frightened— inclined
to move suddenly— how good that feels—
a heat in it— a handful of sugar thrown
on the fire— the tricks we possess
by simply having been here longer—
and knotweed makes a good mother— repetitive—

The still of that smallness— here on the porch—
don't we lose every child in the end?—
no, we don't— today I meant to be writing
about the weather— I mean I take a lot for granted—
like there will always be a metaphor
but knotweed is the same every time—
nothing like words— I mean
to teach my son self-defence—
outdoorsy skills— how to be a survivor—

It occurs to me you might have hurt him
holding on so tight— stilling a child
who meant only to be moving— but everything
we husband is always shedding—
everything has tret— we want to say

13

some things are unnameable—
or some names are unspeakable— but we
are well capable of words—

I've been thinking about knotweed this weather—
knotweed just happens in my head—
knotweed which spreads— makes
the whole world similar— less tangled—
with shoots that taste like rhubarb only better— once
I was a small person and a big person held me—
still— I was frightened— I wanted to know
what would happen— I was moving and I wanted to be held—

Nice

Cockroaches need just
two facts about a place:

how dark
and how many cockroaches.

Or possibly just one fact,
the latter.

A cockroach was the first of us
to give birth in space.

Cockroaches can be fooled
by cockroach-scented robots

into going somewhere bright
where the mind gluts blue.

When the robot
had his mind erased

blue screen blank tape
he trampled the cockroach

but the cockroach
didn't complain.

Robots' legs are
modelled on cockroaches'.

The robot takes the scraps
we've left behind.

He squeeze-boxes
them into building blocks.

He's building a city,
an ode to the city that isn't.

Q: My son wants to know
what happened the city.

A: The summer of 2003
Europe was a fever of heat;

the old died, the young fled
the cities. I knew this girl

so we took off for Nice,
rented a room for next nothing.

What we got
was an addle of roaches.

I pulled my legs up on the chair,
cockroaches waltzing beneath.

Morning after morning,
I took off for the blue.

I swam until the city was gone,
then I floated.

The Car

was black and unwashed
and had fenders.
The windows inclined upwards,
the atmosphere
cool and pure
in all weathers. On sidewalks
a door would fetch open
to bid me ride shotgun,
feet on the dashboard.

A coming-and-going car,
one end
as blunt as the other,
it sawed through a town where
men once built Studebakers,
movie stars stepped out in black and white,
Anna Oliver scolded Henry Ford:
This is a *family* home, Mr Ford.
It wasn't a Chevy
but it was noir.

One night
when you were driving me,
clouds of insects
were ours for outriders.
They died of us and we sang out.
We drove the baby home in that black car.

Stink

They think you came first from Japan
in packing crates
hoping for mulberries, figs and persimmons,

for time to vibrate to one another
come mating season,
one signal longer and lower than any other,

for good sidings and soffits to wander
all winter,
where you'd never let loose the stink of coriander.

First you tried Pennsylvania, then south to Florida
and north to Maine:
you hitched your rides across America.

Dodged jumping spiders and katydids
with eyes for your eggs,
met crickets, ground beetles and earwigs

keen to make you dinner. Learned to prosper
on lima beans,
soya beans, peaches and peppers.

One fall my sister came and erected
a blank sheet
on our deck overnight, a light behind it

to gather bugs. Who was she searching for?
Not you, hibernating
in here with us as though here was where

you'd been headed for. Until the day
we turned up the heat,
making you crazy, blowing your cover.

If you were me, you went out still dreaming
of the words you'd heard
along the road but never hitched to meaning:

Asian pear and *flowering dogwood*,
corn and *cherry* and *apricot tree*.

Umbrella

Look at this couple scooting round the grass;
you can see that he's spoken the rain
so they can hold the umbrella together.

It's not an umbrella, it's a silken manifestation
of something they've talked over and over.
So they parade it before guided tours,

the man with two croissants, the official lovers.
In their slipstream sunshine floats across
blind brick faces, puddles where I stop to cross

the road. It's a creature they're minding, a parallel
universe.
            Later they'll shelve its sinuous objections

and carry the umbrella upstairs to its aquarium.
Kiss it, wish it goodnight, godspeed, slán abhaile.

I love how it moves, so queerly eely through
that briny otherworld in which we can only splash.

Angelus

1

In some forgotten future each displaced caress
must creep home to make its peace with us,
swacked with love it cannot tell from self,

each of the visions that swim at borders
of our dazzled vision must come into focus,
there can be no other end to this. Our city

takes its form from the desert it opposes; we
could settle nowhere else. I write you fetish after fetish,
line them up and toss them, dolls into the oublictte.

2

Such time beats with its own ending, its inlet
its interior, its confident stopping. You followed
signs to steal here, slowed to savour how you are

beloved in this city-not-your-city. Your palms pass over
pointed railings, the leaves of suburban hedges,
a rosary you can't visit on my skin, here, at the centre.

Mouthstrung, we contemplate the surfaces of all things,
two stone monkeys playing pool in the face
of a stone building, for the want of other things.

3

Whenever snow descends from where it hesitates,
　　we begin to talk again about the Rickey, which we may
　　　　not love for the shape it is, but only for the shapes it makes;

whose ballistics drew a device for useless beauty,
　　which portaged air from air to air and back again,
　　　　persistent mechanism of the machine-part city;

　　　　　　how snow is constant in its little heaven
　　　　　　　　above the corner of Michigan and Jefferson
　　　　　　　　　　and burns there indifferent to our existence.

Silver

I need silverfish. Rise cold at night
to cold-cock silverfish. I get a kick
from electric-lighting up their hood.
My husband stomps them with his hand-shoes.
I haven't asked him
if what comes is dust
and he wouldn't tell me if I did.

They've never had the vote. I tell them
once my mum spilled mercury
from a thermometer, balled it
futuristically. She wanted me to think
her girlhood full of mercury and pencil leads
gouged into the balls of hands
of sisters begging for their sisterhood.

She said that where my father worked
the walls were thick with asbestos.
And since my husband's terrified
of poisoning our son,
our bathroom is a fishmoth farm,
cracks spilling silverfish onto infinite white.
They cannot climb. They fear the light.

I've learned the love of silverfish
has three parts. For first
the silverfish stand face to face. Antennae
quiver. They back off and come back.
They think of Roald Dahl, pressing foil on foil
to make a silver ball. Patience is
a thumbnail scoring metal, ironing paper flat.

Then the male makes a dash for it;
the female dashes after.
And when the doctor dashed my son at me,
I could swear he was silver.
Purple, maybe, but silver-gilded:
not a son then, but a monster.
What I remember is gasping and fighting

while my husband fought to sever
the cord, jumping and looping,
that held us together. For thirds
the silverfish are side by side
and head to tail, the male stroking her.
What he gives is wrapped in gossamer.
And now here our silverfish hordes are,

gobbling our discarded skin and hair,
and that is parenthood.
The first silver I found was long before,
a slim string among the hair
issuing from my husband's chest.
We were dirt young then
and I yanked it, threw it to the silverfish.

Postcard of 'Walls of Aran'

in which we learn all Scully's abstractions were just the facts
on the ground   all along   massive to distortion
each shoved full of stone   each elaborate with lichen
sudden blooming by which molluscs survive annihilation
or a child might laugh in Aran   realising of a sudden
that walls are human-fashioned
not eternally drying in scant sun   waiting immemorial
with the apologetic hunch of the giraffe weevil
who would be stunned to learn that grey can exist
like this   an expanse   horny as a lover
who scores notches in the leaf
folds it gently about the next generation   despatches it
with the skill a bloke I fancied brought to skins
on a stone wall   beneath the sky of smoke

Hair

(after Alice Maher's 'Andromeda')

Kind bolus of hair, we who have shoe-horned ourselves
into dream dresses, spooled louis heels down fettled steps

to grooms, or steeled ourselves in suits for the clinch, counter-
signatures gripped in fists; we who have lain on carpets

beside infants, parched for clear shocks of blue, feculence
collecting in our drains, do not forsake us. Domesticated chyme,

damp hank slap-lavished on pillow, pray for us.
We who have fetched home inventing storage solutions,

breaking up space, who feed you and braid you,
scratch compact plans on compact days, give us strength to bear up.

We'd bindle paradise and stow it where the dust bunnies futz,
given leave. Swindle us, please, some less dear salvation.

Croon of nootropics, caffeine, tacit utopia, game feel.
How the way we live days is the means to live lives. Chevy

us through. Tonight, in the kitchens where we make obstacles
of each other, we'll fiddle with the knobs of electrical cookers.

Hobs simulacra for hobs, pixelating heat, steam, spall;
tumble from above as if from nowhere.

Let one of us fright, dash a palm too near. Let flesh char,
hair. Give us our brimstone. Be in our waking.

Mushrooms

Mushrooms could grow on a person all the same.
The body is a vertical farm. Your father and I have begun
a new generation, admitted we didn't have the wits, the brawn.

We've handed on the weather, the body vulnerable and brief,
the fact of mushroom farmers. And there *are* mushrooms, at least,
with names like snakes handled by some Georgia preacher

slick in the arts of faith. There are snake-handlers, who live
dry-bitten by diamondbacks, dealing out chance. There are
scarlet cardinals, flaming out reliably each spring

shriek shriek tut tut tut tut tut. So that even this winter
one might squint at a doily of fern frost, the polar pig's
spore print, and make out something more than a sentence,

might ferret out a night-grown mushroom to whirlygig
in a pocket, fungible chip; might produce Satyr's Beard,
Pheasant's Back, Devil's Urn, as a hipster in downtown

South Bend produces beer, beards, faith in the future of beards;
might trust a body to the blewits. Come to mention
apocalypse (and we can't seem to help it), the way we've lived

this half-dozen years has become our life, as though it had an end.
We tell the night we arrived like myth, thicket of insects' whirr,
throat-thickening heat of the air, impenetrable words

the landlord spoke as he led us up through unlit stairs.
Nights we lay awake in fear, expecting visitors with firearms
and unfamiliar turns of phrase. They'd slaughter us for hesitation.

They elected their first black president that year. We sat snug
on the deck with beers and listened in by lightning bug. How
quickly the strange becomes familiar. How somehow

we got from there to here, bunkered down with you,
American child, in the shrivelights of this cuckoo winter. How
in our time, the weather has changed, and the meaning

of weather. Machines pull machines from a bank of snow, news
is dread-heavy with vortex. They say the way to fix this mess
is to cultivate one's mushrooms and take up very little space.

Instead we want to ask if there might be some way back
to what we wanted when we first came. To flitter about.
Cardinals like bunting. Lightning bugs just lighting out.

A guided tour of the house and its environs

This is where the floor slants   you can roll a ball
This is where I killed the ants with cleaning chemicals
This tortuous shape represents a salamander
squeeze the distance and it grows
it shrinks when we leave it alone

This is where you froze the mouse you'd half-killed
This is where you'll lie down again
with me
I love   your boy shape
I love   'manteltree'
Nobody needs more zombies   Let's not put zombies in the book

These are the crows   or rooks
which gather on the trees around the house
one tree is the tree I imagine swimming in
when I drink too much and sit on the stoop
with you and Michael
or the night I threw the table
as though everything in America had wings

this is where we put the sleeping baby down
for the first time
still in the car seat and watched him

They asked Stein what she thought of the atomic bomb:
'Ms Stein, what do you think of the atomic bomb?'
or she said they did because she was thinking of it

This is where I watched the snow falling
this window   and then this window
On the one hand   and then the other

the way you can count to any number
Later   much later   vitamins will erase the dark circles
                                                    restore the chalk moons

When we woke, sometimes
it was the yellow school bus
already rumbling children
home for lunch, that late

or it was the warning howl
of the freight train
not stopping for anyone, that early

The buses looked more like buses than buses I'd seen
If the river was high things would be expensive   low cheap
Lake effect snow that Christmas and a mad dash for sherry
This is our photograph of Abraham Lincoln
                                            this is a painting my sister made

Here is the beef we ate for the iron   We have been invited
                                                    to a wedding in Austin
Here is the deck the landlord built   Here is our herb garden
Here is my bicycle   You bought a waffle iron

To be honest I usually care quite a lot about the reader but today
I just want to get the whole thing down on paper
                    Even the music we heard on the way to the hospital
                    How I hate the way Americans say 'brava' to women

This is where I entered text into boxes   which sent it
                                                    great distances
This is where   we dismantled America
            before getting back into bed together
if we couldn't have it we said   nobody could

Election Day

A cento

In the architecture of children's dens,
function is subservient to form.

It doesn't matter that a den's loose-ribbed walls
would keep out no winds
or that its entrance can be entered only at a crawl.

When the future was annihilated by the future's arrival,
I was only the father of my son, as if no one were anything but small.

We'll ensure that all can be turned into nothing,
say the polls: we'll lose the capacity to think of nothing,
of not one thing in the world when we are simply being.

People fear repeating a word in the same sentence.
They pause to avoid it superstitiously.

In writing this I notice the care it costs not to use certain words.
I write this not to mention the future,
or to speak of the architecture of dens,

but to let my son know
that if he ever wonders what he's done –

and everyone does wonder, sooner or later –
he has been grace to me.
It may seem to him no great thing

to have been the child of a man in a den of blankets.
If only I had leaves to build a heatless fire.

Postcards from Europe

1

Our paper lanterns are not flares but sparks
off some imagined bonfire while somewhere

Europe dreams of burning, dreams of bombs
that will be sent off here and there, piercing

light, their history a history of staring
into fire. Europe dreams of burning,

dreams of bombs. A bomb is made, in part,
of light, of visits to the cinema, where Paris,

made of light, must be annihilated first.
Our lanterns are not flares but sparks.

Here the harvest's in, the children witness
to corn's absence in the field, the quince trees

stripped of all their quinces. Europe dreams of
burning, dreams of bombs. We sing and see

St Martin on his horse, a vision of the strangeness
little children swim in, beneath the light of stars.

Beneath the stars, the light of us. Our paper lanterns,
swinging as we walk, are not flares but sparks

off some imagined bonfire while somewhere
Europe dreams of burning, dreams of bombs.

2

Crossing the border between Hungary and Romania,
travelling and destination, outside and in,
was a sword swallowing act.
He was a small man on a tall stool
with feathered wings tattooed on his back.
He crowed a spiel about putting money in his hat,
shocking the children in the audience:
If a man can swallow the whole blade of a sword,
should we not fête him as the doer of feats,
pay all his bills, give him a place at court?

First you must overcome the gag reflex.
You must learn to breathe in without breathing out.
Line up the muscles of your gut,
make of your mouth a gin trap.
The thing slides in quite slowly,
take it to the hilt.
Your throat becomes the rut for the runners of a sleigh,
your tonsils lean to lick at it,
the metal of your fillings sings,
your tongue tastes the cold, a long, cold drink.
Fillings singing like blades in a drawer, the train entering a tunnel,
things that go where they belong, belong where they are,
a carp's scale in a shepherd's purse,
the sword is gone.

Children wonder at the trick.
They wonder that an adult hasn't clapped hands over their eyes,
sent them to bed.
They wonder at the man passing round a hat, what it will take
to make their lives heroic.
The border police came and went.
The train was like the Orient Express
and we shared our compartment with a Romanian
coming home from a student union meeting in Prague.

3

Beneath the floating railway
the ghosts of horses sweat light.
They were to be, they were never to be.
How they swam the length
of the Wupper in the conditional
we'll never know.
                    One day the monorail
will give birth to an elephant, a perfect execution
docked for want of a springboard.
Recall the unfair decision, a half-century
earlier, to value grace and ease
over difficult failure
in plunging forth.
                    Emperor Wilhelm II,
palsy akimbo, will ace his own stunt
on the Schwebebahn, who years before
chomped the leg of Uncle Alfred
Duke of Edinburgh,
as Edison chomped the phonograph.
No doubt to sink a hold on these vibrations
that issue constantly forth
and constantly fold back on us.
                    Suspended above Wuppertal,
swooping left and right,
how we might holler, spared the breath for it!
How we might insist on going around again,
on none of this business of history
having anything to do with itself.

Service Not Included

(Dundrum)

Who's to thank for the buckets of lavender thrown open beside us,
for the foam-clouds on twin cappuccinos,
for the carved boxes that hold sugar,
for the child telling reams about superheroes,
for the darkening sky of the waiter,
at a café in the shopping centre
when you cannot speak for your tears?
Hospital coffee was never so kindly, so quick to make believe.
On the morning I wed, you and I
came here to the shopping centre
and scented women pared our nails in a scented room.
Who's to thank for their cool hands
working away in our memories? Here, your hands
are out of my reach. You must have thought it, but,
when my son was born howling and writhing
and thrust to my skin, how your own son left the room
and the snap they left you to hold of him. Your hands
are smaller than mine, and neat.
How they told you the hospital name and you thought
that dun square of Monopoly board,
made your way there by a route you'd score
into your palms by the end; saved change
for the car park; packed a Thermos, perhaps.
Now families glide about the shopping centre
in neons fresh from invention, eyes shiny with gratitude,
music tasteful and tender.
You must have thought, when my son has made strange,
raged at being made come asunder,
of all the times you had to leave the hospital
and drive home to your daughters.

Of all the skin we need to touch and are not touched,
of all the starving to the touch, the familiar injustices.
Spread coins thick across the tables,
go about the shopping centre,
praise the coffee, the kindness of the escalator, haircuts,
the beautiful, the beautiful, the familiar,
the comfortable weather. Who's to thank? Who's to
praise for your hands, who sits up there in head office
taking our minds off the past waiting rooms and coffee docks?

Jellyfish

At first you only noticed one—
a translucent crisp nestling in the sand—
the perfectly circular ghosts of its gonads—
and recalled another summer's plump
and gloating—

Then you took in death's full
murmuration on the strand— slug-pocked
with the dried-up sucker-marks—
                                    child—
bossing your brother and sister around—
                        did you step on one crisp jellyfish?

Barefoot— as if experimentally—

As if in the constellation
                there existed some design—
        the sketch of a map—
                your child's face mapped on the sand—

Parents—
who'll be old when your child is young—
one rummaging— one naked under a towel—
a brother and sister running around—
                        your responsibility—
        a castle of sand— a wet dog— an enormous sky—
all of it as if mutely—

        You lay in the bottom bunk
of the bunk bed
        of the second room

                    of the holiday house
                            by the yellow strand—
        dreaming of faces—

                    loomy and foamy—

a dream the previous child had left in the bed—
or a dream oozing down from your sister—
or only because in the past
            you haven't met your future—
                so naturally your child's face is unfamiliar—

You'll bring your child to the beach
and build a castle of sand— your child
            looks like you— greedy smile—
                    eyes splayed in thought

You'll steal from other poets
            the haystack- and roof-levelling wind—
                    the sea-wind—
                            the sea's murderous innocence—
            where slugs with their slime-trails
are porous as mirrors—

Where ice— far away but you can't help
            knowing about it—
                    calves and crashes—

Where comb jellies— far away but you can't help
            knowing about it—
                    spawn deliriously

Where plastics— far away but you can't help
            knowing about it—
                    make an island—

Where ancient air— far away but you can't help
        knowing about it—
                is released from pockets—

Some jellyfish have motors—
        some can choose to grow younger—
                a jellyfish is a lens too slippery to hold to an eye—

You happen on them again
        in the future
                in their hundreds—

Swimming or not swimming
they must have come
        mooning with intention
                from your keepnet—

 your child moves with a shovel
        to sling them back into the sea—

Once you saw a photograph
of a child—
        lifeless—
                on a beach—

so did everybody

After my son was born

I'd a snip cut in his tongue.
Blood scissored down his chin.
At every squall I'd been unsnibbing
myself and starving him. He knocked
me so my nose coughed blood,
punched a finger through my cornea.
Blood blubbed on my nipple
where his gums met. On the radio
somebody was saying something about Syria.
My son jerked knots of hair from my head,
tears dashed off his fontanelle. He'd fixed
my hips so my clothes didn't fit. I blundered
him once against the door-jamb:
blood. I'd bit his father
when we were younger, drinking harder,
made blood come then. Twice I tried to leave
him screaming, twenty minutes at a time,
but couldn't keep schtum.
One breakfast I broke the mug that insisted
'Don't Mess With Texas.'
Smashed it. And all the time
I smiled so much my teeth dried.
He made everything heavy.
Like they say the bomb did for a while,
so that Americans swam
through their homes, eyes peeled,
picking up everyday things and dropping them
as though they were violated with light and pain.
As though blood hadn't always been there, waiting.

After my son was born

grit shone on the surfaces
of my bedazzled eyes.

Flesh pooled about me,
so that it was difficult to run.

Disease squeaked an entrance
at the corners of window frames,
the gap beneath the door, my
shut mouth.

I wished you all dead.

After my son was born,
my mother came to me
and was gentle.

ALPHABET

for Inger Christensen

1

apricot trees insist; apricot trees insist

2

but brand-names insist; and battlefields, battlefields;
bombs still insist; and blackface, and blackface

3

concrete insists; cappuccinos, cathedrals;
cancer-treatment centres, electric cigarettes,
corn syrup, cattle prods, automated cash machines

4

death-bringers insist, dreamcatchers and dolls;
drones insist, and daffodil hybrids, daffodil hybrids;
drills, derricks and data insist; dust storms
and dust events; drone deaths and dental dams,
online dating sites and death squads

5

early morning insists, eely hour, evilling hour;
Einsamkeit und Engeln, uaigneas agus aingil;
dreams of widowhood and elk, half fled, insist;
Europe nestling in an elbow's crook, too abstract
at this hour; eider feathers insist; every
possibility insists, each future history,
here beneath our eiderdowns with earnest breath
earth insists its way into our future

6

flashmobs insist, with their fleeting
raid on community, the flash a fire
that frees through them and fades;
in cities they insist, in what we flatter
public space; foreplay insists, and forecourts, foreclosures;
flatbreads, flatmates, and flatpack furniture;
flowcharts and the funds of financial advisors;
errors insist: instrumental, random,
systemic; flexitime insists, and fuchsia;
and fruit still insists, fruit here in the supermarket where
somewhere apricot trees exist, apricot trees exist;
the weight of fuzzed flesh forthright in a palm;
the five-finger discount still insists

7

given prickles insist, given prickles,

yellow-gemmed, grizzly,
going where the ground gives itself

generously, greedily, giddily,
geometries ginnelling into galaxies,

the gambrels made by generation,
the grimoire hatching woody riddles,
the darkening thatch of glossary

growing in our wildernesses;
gadabouts seeking getaways,
for whom given limits don't insist;

we inherit only what we generate;
but grief insists on itself, grief moves by whim,
grief would be a fire break;
but fire fans grief; and grief feeds caterpillars,
homes stonechat, yellowhammer, linnet;

low-growing where the ground is bare
enigmatic as the gun I give
my child to gloss, grip right, handle;
little goose, blonde gunsel;
when grief's out of blossom, kissing's out of fashion

8

human remains insist, human remains insist
on whispering a last hyacinth, one last honeyed hiss

sinking back into hollows and hidey-holes,
their holy places, softnesses and hardnesses,
hummocks losing height, hips unhanded a half-life

here in places where there once sproinged hair,
happened wetnesses, quick havings, slow hallelujahs;
where a man laboured on pleasure with his two hands;

how it dawned on us what the happenings in my body meant;
how we lay and waited to know what to say;
how at last we confessed we wanted this;
how little more we could say about it;
how the heat of others made me want to heave;

how my boss said that when his wife went to the obstetrician he
        wanted to hit the obstetrician;
how the pain only let up when I crawled on the sitting-room floor;
how the pain only let up when I swam in the city pool;
how the happening was a cat on my lap I could never throw off;
how the obstetrician said on Monday he would hoist the human out;

how he said no breakfast but I had nectarines and coffee;
how we listened to TC love his honeybear;
how the receptionist said I was ready to pop;
how we hardly had to wait for the nurse to hook me up;
and Pitocin insists, Pitocin insists
on hypnotising the body,
Charcot's hands making the drawing passes,
hexing away my objections to any of this;

and hospitals insist, charts hang insistence
on the ends of hospitable beds,
hospital gowns insist and hospital breakfasts; a card insists
I feed him x times before they'll bathe him; a nurse insists
I try placing this small contraption;
they dress him before I insist on his nakedness;
the hospital hat doesn't fit him; they bathe him insisting;
he insists all night long but only I hear him

9

still, I insist, I insist
he exists, a child
I'll ruin slowly,

he inks his own skin
when distressed, an idiosyncrasy,
meaningless difference insists
but he's the spit of his granny,
has yet to learn ice sculptures exist

coaxed like ice wine
from iterations of impatience
and determination, condemned
to exist, to drip; it isn't really
about the end of everything, this;

it's about iterations
by which living
becomes more difficult
until unbearable by intervals
in which nonetheless we will persist;
about interesting times
and isness and how indeed
I will insist, I intend to insist,

although I have no control over it, the ice and its drip,
I intend it for my child, his dear irrelevance,
I intend kingfisher's ice and chrome yellow irises,
I intend him ice cream sandwiches
in a calm interior, small garden included;
it's not unreasonable, I have an income,
I can buy ice cream, pay rent, earn interest;
so I refuse, I reject the ice cap's insistence;

although Icarus wrapped in the melting wax
wings insists; Icarus in that split second
before the fall still as a hatchet fish;
Icarus high as a kite, blank with the no-going-back of it;
this being his one interval of lambency
between blank and blank, this being
his only version of existence, his brief island,
I insist he will milk it, I insist
on the ice in his eyes, the light in his irises;
Icarus-child spoiling like milk
in the glut of my insistence,
eat ice cream, pull the legs off insects,
strum instruments, ink intensely;

we will insist, small as pollen spores in ice,
intimate as bones, isolated as the great
blue whale's hum we read about each night
at storytime, little Icarus in your high bunk,
we'll insist; I'm with you in it;
I'm insisting, spread your arms, bend your knees;
ice bears exist, and eiderdown quilts;
lengthen your back and lower your head;
iridescent wings exist and ispíní;
take a deep breath and say your alphabet;
splay your feet like the bittern stepping and booming
in among the marsh plants of the buffering internet:
isn't this enough? Isn't this sufficient?

10

in some places July nights insist;
there's our deck in July in mid-America,
its swing seat, its beers, its biting insects;
you and I do injustice to all the July
nights of other places since;

as though nowhere were July
but in mid-America where
the bats' ears of jade turn
towards the ticking haze;
I read of the past jury of months
that each has been the hottest
version of itself on record
and think only of that July

I was heaviest, each morning
folding heat I'd gathered by night
into the water of the pool adjacent to you
so that all the rest of our lives
we are a little jealous of ourselves
in that interval perfectly repeated,
July mornings following July nights
in the jotter-blank pool,

jet-headed you, me in my jet-black swimsuit,
within my belly the baby, the budding judge,
knee-joints kicking,
swinging his tiny jambs,
swimming the jammy mulch,
already sporting the tiny fore-jacket,
already yakking his jaw, the oldest bone,
already insisting, already jonesing,

already jimmying the lock;
then at night cold drinks and lightning bugs,
routine being a kind of jubilation;
a person could say your head was jet,
a person could say your eyes were jade,

a person could speak of joy in loving you;
a person could jumble life with you with life on earth,
no joke, a person could insist on jumbling it;
could insist on the deck and the lightning bugs,
on the bats turning their jade ears,
on the slow jabber of our chat and its gaps,
on the jewel from the mall on my ring finger,
on the jointed boy incubating in my belly and forget

we are not doomed yet

juggle the numbers

some are doomed
but not the 3 of us

or not the 3 of us
just yet

or maybe 1 of us,
the smallest,

the 1 of us
still learning
numbers,

who doesn't know
what 2 of us
are keeping to ourselves:

that 2 of us
will hie out of here
leaving 1 of us

to fend;
so I stand
in the kitchen

cooking for the 3
of us, keeping
the future to myself;

the part I like best is
the chopping,
1 onion or 1 pepper,

how it yields more
than it promises,
1 bell pepper
is the right number
for 3 of us,

I recall how you
stand before the tap,
reddening knuckles,
turning 1 spud
beneath water,
letting the children

who are playing
just about be heard,
letting the jackdaws
who are calling
just about be heard,

letting the larches
who are whispering
just about be heard,
letting the silence
just about be heard

11

kin insists, kin insists;
your pink cheek tucked up
with mine, not thinking
of solitude or extinction,
of the whale in your book,

not thinking of the pink krill
with intricate eyes; not thinking
of kelp forking over rocks,
their thick holdfasts, fat
kelp picked for iodine; not thinking

of the parakeets in city parks,
brilliant-greened, ring-necked,
flocking insistence,
shrieking insistence,
over the clack of the woodpeckers,
over the tick of the bracken,
reckoning with falcon;
not thinking of the quickening

catkins on the tree outside,
not thinking of elk
somewhere in America, not
thinking of the blackberries
you picked and cooked
with your papa, of spillikin oaks,
of silkworms killed
for their cocoons,

of kingfishers, of quaking grass,
of knotgrass and rock doves,

of kale patches
in some difficult aftermath,
never thinking of elm keys
falling like manna, or
how it might look
when an apricot tree quickens,

not thinking of the grubs
beneath barkskin,
mackerel shoals
or eider ducks; thinking
only of your pink cheek

and mine, tucked up together

your nakedness was always
quick as a kiss
licking the house,
a cuckoo flash,
little war path
at the limit of my vision;
all it takes is a kink
in my attention

and you are taken;
all at once
your lack insists;
maybe you are taken by a kiss
or a fuck from a sick lover,
jerking as a bird drinks water;
maybe you are suffocated
by spiking heat
and cannot make protest;
taken by the vitamins
not in your food, the muck
your vegetables grow in;
maybe knotweed tucks away

your body, insists on it;
maybe you are taken
by whatever's hidden
in the silky water
slaking your old-fashioned thirst;
by fake drugs or skin dressed up
to take you in; by crackling flames
or darkness when the fuel
gives out or soaks through;
maybe you are taken by another person
angry and broken when scarcity thickens;
the click of the trigger
one morning when you have

something to take; stroke; heart attack;
maybe you don't make it
far enough for any of that;

somewhere you are suddenly born
into an expressionless house;
when you try to speak

the walls won't hold
and the garden, which
I promised you,

is eaten by the slugs
you used to want to stroke,
slow and black,

make pets, love; the fruit
we meant to pickle
our first winter here

is eaten; the ground
sick with dust, the trees
sick; you peel off some dusty

tree bark, you dig up a bulb
to eat; the walls won't hold;
you walk in the streets,

do as others do, kick
what pieces of brick
come before you;

where the route sticks
the buildings don't hold;
the wilderness streaks

in every direction;
a shock of July
in the wrong bit of calendar

somewhere perhaps you meet
that apricot tree,
its forking branches,

its veiled expression, its
thinly-veiled cankers, before
walking on regardless

I'll look for you here; okay,
makes more sense I think
than looking at the sky;
than harking in church,
tucking heels, marking time;
okay, makes more sense
than flicking through books,
plucking echoes, tracking words;

makes more sense;
okay, so this is where I look;
I poke beneath bracken;
bracken makes a blanket
for huckleberries;
bracken makes a hide for the skylark;
there's no panicking in here;
bracken does our thinking for us,
taking in time and making a nest; okay,
taking in love; bracken
has its own clock, its own ticking,
bracken wakes the sunshine,
darkens rain for the black

slug to take it here and there; okay,
bracken eking its way like a canker;
bracken where flukes of snow resist light,
its green flicks multiplying, ticking spores
dusty with sickness, okay, but think
of the prayer crooked in here;
think of the echoes marking time;
think of the huckleberries, the skylark
waking and thinking, the sunshine hiding
and thinking, the rain ticking and thinking;
think what's taken in, given nook;
bracken making sense for us; okay,
so this is where I look.

NOTES

Still (13)
This poem was written as part of a translation game curated by Ricarda Vidal and Maria-José Blanco. It draws on Sam Knight's essay 'The Day of the Knotweed: Battling Britain's most destructive plant' (*Harper's Magazine*, May 2015).

The Car (17)
For a significant part of the 20th century, the Oliver family and the Studebaker family were the major employers in South Bend, Indiana, manufacturing ploughs and cars respectively.

Angelus (21)
The line in italics adapts a phrase from Italo Calvino's *Invisible Cities*, translated by William Weaver (Harcourt Brace Jovanovich, 1974). The 'Rickey' of the poem is 'Two Planes: Vertical Horizontal IV', a kinetic sculpture by George Rickey on permanent display in South Bend, where he was born.

Silver (24)
Roald Dahl describes his ball of chocolate wrappers in *Going Solo* (Jonathan Cape, 1986).

Postcard of 'Walls of Aran' (26)
The postcard comes from an exhibition of Sean Scully's work at the National Gallery of Ireland.

Mushrooms (28)
This poem was written at the home of Rachel Swenie, who farms mushrooms in Chicago. The 'polar pig' or 'polar vortex' was a period of extraordinarily cold weather which hit the American Midwest in 2014.

Postcards from Europe (33)
The suspended monorail at Wuppertal is the oldest of its kind in the world. When it was first built, it was assumed that other cities would follow suit; it was a prototype for the future. The elephant's name was Tuffi.

Jellyfish (38)

I had in mind Karl Mathiesen in *The Guardian*, 21 August 2015: 'Like a karmic device come to punish our planetary transgressions, jellyfish thrive on the environmental chaos humans create. Is the age of the jellyfish upon us?' And jellyfish expert Peter Richardson in the same article: 'Are the jellyfish trying to tell us something?'

Alphabet (43)

'Alphabet' is based on *alphabet* by Inger Christensen, as translated into English by Susannah Nied (Bloodaxe Books, 2000). Christensen's poem begins with the line 'apricot trees exist, apricot trees exist' and ends with the atom bomb. It is an abecedarian, but with a twist: the number of lines in each section is dictated by the Fibonacci sequence, in which each number is the sum of the two previous numbers. While the alphabet is a human construction, the Fibonacci sequence is inevitable, since it is found in nature. Christensen claims not to have known the Fibonacci sequence was a natural one when she wrote *alphabet* – an example, perhaps, of the poem knowing more than the poet.